MW00884378

The Struggle Is Real but God's Grace Is Life-Changing

Bible Study Stories and Prayer Devotionals about Deliverance, Divine Intervention and Supernatural Turnarounds

By Lynn R Davis

Published By

Lynn R. Davis

Copyright © 2017 All rights reserved.

No part of this publication may be copied, reproduced in any format, by any means, electronic or otherwise, without prior consent from the copyright owner and publisher of this book.

Three times I pleaded with the lord about this, that it should leave me. But he said to me, "my grace is sufficient for you, for my power is made perfect in weakness." Therefore I will boast all the more gladly of my weaknesses, so that the power of Christ may rest upon me.

2 Corinthians 12:8-9

CONTENTS

The Struggle Is Real but God's Grace

Is Life-Changing

Bible Study Stories and Prayer Devotionals
about Deliverance, Divine Intervention and

Supernatural Turnarounds

By Lynn R Davis

Want Free E-books? Register your email
address at **IMotivateMyself.com**

Psalm 46: 1-3

*God is our refuge and strength an ever-
present help in trouble. Therefore we will
not fear, though the earth give way, and the
mountains fall into the heart of the sea,
though its waters roar and foam, and the
mountains quake with their surging. Selah*

STRUGGLE. A forceful or violent effort to get free of restraint or resist attack.

Is Struggle the New Black?

I look around nowadays and I see a lot of struggle. I've seen *the struggle is real* printed on t-shirts and coffee mugs. A simple Google image search and tons of memes glorifying the struggle sprawl across your screen. It's catchy; it's memorable; and most of all, everyone can relate in some way.

Some people say it in jest; others are seriously fighting to survive. Wrestling against fear, depression, divorce, illness, disappointment, you name it. Maybe that's you.

You're worried and afraid or just plain frustrated. The bad news is your struggles are real. The good news is God's grace is all-powerful.

You are not your fears, worries, or insecurities. You may be experiencing these struggles, but they do not define you. You are defined by God.

God of Abraham, Isaac, and Jacob, who parted the red sea and raise Jesus from the dead, He is your God.

The God who is bigger than your struggle and He loves you infinitely and immeasurably.

So much that He has given you Grace. Free, no strings attached favor that flows to you 24 hours a day 7 days a week, whether you deserve it or not. You can't buy it. You can't lose it. You can't overuse it.

If you are tired of struggling, this Grace is for you. You're exhausted and you want better, this Grace is for you. All you need is a little encouragement and divine direction to keep you going until your change comes. That's where I come in. I was the struggle queen. If it was a struggle, I had it.

Because of that, I feel your pain. I know the struggle, and I can encourage you with a sincere heart from the perspective of an ex-struggler.

My aim is always the same in my books, to offer support and raise your hopes. This is the second book I've written about struggles. If you haven't read, *How God*

Sees Your Struggles, I encouraged you to do so.

I wrote it as God helped me through the struggle of a relationship disaster. Maybe you can relate to those.

The last Amazon review I read described it as, *"One of the most helpful and reassuring books I've read in a long time."*

I love reading comments like that- goal achieved, thank you, Jesus.

I think it's also helpful to so many because it's about developing a fresh perspective that can give you life. And changing your perspective for the better is the beginning of transformation- another new buzz word- *transformation.*

The struggle may be real, but never let any struggle become more real than your Almighty Creator.

Hebrews 12:1 says, "Wherefore seeing we also are compassed about with so great a cloud of witnesses, let us lay aside every weight and the sin which doth so easily beset us, and let us run with patience the race that is set before us,"

Struggles don't just come once in life. They come again and again and again. You can find something beautiful in the struggle, but boy is it sometimes difficult to uncover. 99.9% of it is perspective. You're probably tired of hearing that. I know I was.

Some Objectives for *The Struggle Is Real*

You're going to enjoy this, I promise. This book is many things. It's a bit like a bible study. Somewhat of a devotional and contains a few elements of a prayer book. All geared toward helping the reader not just overcome struggle, but showing you that struggle is an opportunity in disguise.

I pray by the time you complete this book you believe with all your heart that God:

Has *already* given you what you need to endure and overcome the struggle (GRACE).

It is and all ways will be bigger than your struggle.

Will turn your struggle into a pathway for success.

Has equipped you with everything you need to overcome the struggle. You can transform your struggles into success.

It's not always easy to get through a struggle, but the rewards at the end out of it are out of this world-literally. I enjoyed writing this. You're going to love reading it.

If you take these lessons to heart, you're going to wake up with a new attitude every morning. The message is life-changing and once you get it- there's no stopping you.

You had Grace yesterday, you have Grace today and you'll have Grace tomorrow. Feel that. Believe it. And the next time you see struggle coming say, *bring it on, I got this!*

IN HIS GRACE IS CONFIDENCE

Let us have confidence, then, and approach God's throne, where there is grace. There we will receive mercy and find grace to help us just when we need it.

Hebrews 4:16

~CHAPTER 1 ~

RUN AND TELL THAT

(DANIEL 3)

THE STRUGGLE GOT HEATED FOR SHADRACH, MESHACH, AND ABED-NEGO.

You may know this story, but for those who do not, I will summarize. Besides, this story inspires me so much, I'm happy to tell it over and over again.

It all started when King Nebuchadnezzar got the bright idea to build a ninety-foot gold statue. He scheduled a dedication and invited all the dignitaries and officials. On the day that everyone gathered,

Nebuchadnezzar proclaimed, "People of all languages when you hear the music, you must fall and worship the golden image. Whoever does not will immediately be thrown into a fiery furnace."

So the next time the music played everyone stopped and bowed to worship this idol. Everyone that is, except Shadrach, Meshach, and Abednego. Some of the King's "loyal" subjects (aka haters) observed their refusal to bow. Immediately, they ran to tell the king. Gladys Kravits had nothing on them. They saw it all and told it all.

Now Run and Tell That

There are people around you who are loyal to the world's system. They're loyal to gossip. They're loyal to backstabbing and betrayal. They watch you. The instant you miss a step they are going to run and tell any and everyone who will listen.

But don't let that worry you. As you're about to see, God can use them to bless you.

Before the reporters began their tattle-tale mission, they reminded the King of his decree:

[10] You, O king, have made a decree that everyone who hears the sound of the horn, flute, harp, lyre, *and* psaltery, in symphony with all kinds of music, shall fall and worship the gold image; [11] and whoever does

not fall and worship shall be cast into the midst of a burning fiery furnace.

No doubt jealousy probably played a part since the King had placed the Hebrew boys in positions of power.

Anytime God places you in a position of power, there is always someone lurking in the shadows hoping that you make mistake so that they can pull you down.

I've learned even when you don't think you have anything to envy, you're still subject to the enemy because you have something the enemy doesn't have.

You have the grace and favor and they know. They may not know exactly what it is, but they know there's something special about the way you operate.

The enemy sees your favor, even if you don't. They see your potential and pray that you do not. They see how you worship God and blessing flow into your life because of it. They're crabs in a barrel clawing their way to the top. Yet, all you seem to do is pray and believe.

They don't understand you've got Grace.

You don't have to bow to any ungodly image, false god; or ungodly person. With God, you can stand the heat. The God you serve is well able to protect you and provide for you. The weapon might form, but it won't prosper. The struggle may get heated, but it will not consume you.

The struggle is real, but you have God's Grace. Don't buckle under pressure. Let them run and tell. Keep serving your God. Keep praying night and day. Keep lifting holy hands toward heaven and watch what God will do.

Those men must have felt satisfaction at first. They thought they'd accomplished something. The people in your life, who betrayed you, think they're doing something. They may feel some satisfaction now, but little do they know God will use them to give you a platform. God will use their ill-will for your good.

"Is it true, Shadrach, Meshach, and Abednego, that you will not bow down and worship the image of gold that I have made? Just in case there was a mistake I will give you another chance. When the music plays again you will be ready and bow down to the image, and if you don't this time you will be thrown into a fiery furnace. Then what god will be able to save you?"

Struggles Expose the Enemy

The struggle that was designed to destroy you will do the opposite. It will expose your enemies and set you up for success in the process.

When King Nebuchadnezzar heard the report, he got so angry that he called for the three men so that he could confront them. Shadrach, Meshach, and Abednego must have stunned the crowd when they answered:

"…O Nebuchadnezzar, we do not need to defend ourselves before you in this matter. (17) If we are thrown into the blazing furnace, the God we serve can save us from it, and he will rescue us from your hand, O King. (18)But even if He does not, we want you to know, O King that we will not serve your gods or worship the image of gold you have set up."

This is more drama than Law & Order, CSI, and The Good Wife all rolled together. I'd always remembered that they didn't bow down, but I never gave much thought to what they said. Not only did they refuse to bow, but they also didn't even feel a need to defend themselves. As far as they were concerned there was nothing to discuss.

We have to reach a point in the struggle where we are unbothered by the circumstances. Failure is not even up for discussion, "God forbid: yea, let God be true, but every man a liar; (Romans 3:4)

God's word is the truth. He knows the beginning from the end (Is. 46:10). He is the God of victory and breakthrough. He's going to deliver us and if things don't go the way we want them to, guess what?

We're still going to serve Him because all things work together for the good of them who love the Lord and are called according to His purpose (Romans 8:28).

That's what Shadrach, Meshach, and Abed-Nego's said to King Nebuchadnezzar. They didn't blink, stutter, or flinch. That's struggle-is-real-but-so-is-my-God-faith.

There's nothing worse than having an audience when you go through a struggle. Eyes on your day and night watching to see what you are going to do and how you're going to respond. No one is offering any good advice or help, they're just spectators. But remember to keep in mind, God can turn your struggle into a platform.

He's promised to prepare a table in the presence of your enemies. So you have to have enemies for this promise to come to pass, right?

Who's In Your Circle?

Shadrach, Meshach, and Abednego stood together. There is no indication that either of them wavered in their resolve. Scripture tells us *wherever two or three are gathered touching and agreeing, He will be in the midst.*

In a struggle, there is one thing you want to be crystal clear about- Who has your back. We need to know the people in our circle and where they stand. One of the worst feelings is to be in the middle of a struggle and find out that someone you thought was your friend turned out to be an enemy.

Someone you thought was strong turned out to be the weakest link.

To activate the *Principle of Agreement* you need to be with people who think and believe as you do. If two or three of you can and pray together on one accord for God's glory to touch your situation and turn it around, God has promised that He will show up. I dropped the ball on this principle when I was married. Ego and hurt feelings got in the way.

People who desire reconciliation have to pray and understand that it only works if you put aside your differences long enough to stand in agreement. Acknowledge the wrong; make an apology for the mistakes; change the behavior; show each other respect, and stand in agreement.

Turn It Up!

By this time in the story, you could have fried an egg on King Nebuchadnezzar's head. The Hebrew boys had defied his authority in front of everyone. He had to make an example of them. So instead of just throwing them into the furnace, he had the guards turn it up ten times normal. It was so hot, the soldiers who threw the Hebrew boys in, were burned to death.

No doubt feeling proud of himself, King Nebuchadnezzar looked inside the furnace, but His haughty spirit was crushed when he saw that they were walking around unbound and without so much as a blister. And to top it off, they weren't alone.

"Weren't there only three men thrown into the fire?" They replied, "O, yes king." He said, "Look! I see four men walking around in the fire, untied and unhurt, and the fourth looks like some kind of angel!"

Your struggle may be real, but don't you know that God can unbind you? You can't stand for God and be forsaken. No matter how blistering your struggle may seem to the people on the outside of the furnace, on the inside, you have Christ Jesus, the Lord, and Savior who in you has set your free indeed and the gates of hell cannot prevail against you!

When the King called for Shadrach, Meshach, and Abednego to come out of the furnace, he said, "follower of the Highest God, come out!"

He recognized immediately that their God is Almighty. Whether he liked it or not, he had to recognize that these men must serve a God who is almighty.

When people see you walking around in your struggles, unbound, they're going to have to recognize that the God you serve, is the Most High God!

God will turn your struggle into a platform just like he did for the three men in the furnace. Their enemies were encamped about them, but they feared no evil because the Lord was with them. He comforted them. He prepared a platform in the presence of their enemies!

By the end of this story, even King Nebuchadnezzar revoked his old decree; instituted a new one; and gave the three men better positions than they had previously held.

When God gets involved, He makes sure that you come out better than when you went in. And the people around you can't help but give God the glory because they've been watching you the entire time and they know it couldn't have been anything other than God's power that brought you out.

Even the people who tried to hold you back will have to serve your God. Romans 14:11, says, "As surely as I live,' says the Lord, 'every knee will bow before me; every tongue will acknowledge God

#TSIR, but so is your God.

LESSONS FROM THE HEBREW BOYS' STRUGGLE ~

*God doesn't always take us out of the struggle.

Sometimes he comes in to help us get through it.

*Don't fret over people who are out to get you.

*Keep the faith and believe that

*God will give you favor that will lead to something better.

*You have to have enemies to have a table prepared before them.

~ MY PRAYER ~

I declare, in the name of Jesus, I will not be consumed in the fire. The enemy's plans to harm me are destroyed. No weapon formed shall prosper. Every stronghold is broken. In the name of Jesus, I am unbound and free indeed. No harm comes to me.

Every knee shall bow before Jehovah-Jireh. My enemies bow before you God, El Shaddai. They acknowledge and confess my God is the one true God. He is Elohim.

My struggle is real, but my God has already created a way of escape. This struggle will not destroy me. God will use it to create a platform that will exalt His kingdom's work and cause me to be promoted.

The authority is mine in the name of Jesus. Whatever I bind on earth is bound in heaven and whatsoever I loose on earth shall be loosed in heaven. In Jesus' name, the struggle is finished. Praise God!

~ TRANSFORMATIONAL SCRIPTURES

 *Daniel 3:28-Then Nebuchadnezzar said, "Praise be to the God of Shadrach, Meshach, and Abednego, who has sent his angel and rescued his servants! They trusted in him and defied the king's command and were willing to give up their lives rather than serve or worship any god except their own God".

 *Daniel 4: 3-How great are his signs, how mighty his wonders! His kingdom is eternal; his dominion endures from generation to generation.

 *Daniel 4: 34-At the end of that time, I, Nebuchadnezzar, raised my eyes toward heaven, and my sanity was restored. Then I praised the Highest; I honored and glorified him who lives forever.

 *Daniel 6:26- I issue a decree that in every part of my kingdom people must fear and reverence the God of Daniel. For he is the living God and he endures forever; his kingdom will not be destroyed, his dominion will never end.

 `*`

IN HIS GRACE IS STRENGTH

But the grace that God gives is even
stronger. As the scripture says, "God resists
the proud, but gives grace to the humble."
James 4:6

~CHAPTER 2 ~

PAIN WITH A PURPOSE

(Genesis 37)

THE STRUGGLE WAS REAL FOR JOSEPH, THE SON OF JACOB. Joseph, at age 17, began having dreams that he was a ruler. He shared those dreams with his family. But, they dismissed them as nonsense. His brothers were already jealous because their father, Jacob loved Joseph best and his dreams only made matters worse.

The more he shared his dreams, the more he was hated. Your dreams will either attract supporters or expose adversaries.

Joseph's brothers plotted to kill him, all but one, Reuben talked them into just throwing Joseph in a deep pit (Genesis 37:22). Reuben had interceded, but Joseph didn't know that. All he saw was a pit with no ladder- a pit with no way out.

He couldn't see the favor. Maybe you can't see the favor either. Dear friend, you are still alive. That's a favor. You may be in the pit of struggle with no way out, but as long as you're alive, there is an opportunity to survive and by faith, in your season, you will thrive.

Jesus is interceding on your behalf (Romans 8:34). Angels are encamped about you ready to lift you (Psalm 91:12) in your struggle. The Lord is always there.

Joseph's struggles came one after the other. He went from pit to slavery to prison. Just when he thought the pit experience was behind him and things were looking up with his boss; he ran into another problem (Potiphar's wife). He'd thought it couldn't get any worse, but then he landed in prison.

Have you ever felt like you were continually making two steps forward and ten steps back? I know I have on several occasions. You find yourself thinking, "*Seriously God, is this ever going to end?*"

Take heart, though the devil planned to kill you, God has favored you. You won't be destroyed. Not on God's watch. Great things lie ahead for you.

What about the bad stuff? Why would God plan that? Struggles have a way of making us question ourselves and unfortunately our God. We cannot possibly understand everything. I don't pretend to.

I don't believe that every struggle is orchestrated by God, but I do believe that He is with us in every one. One thing I've come to understand though is this- *even if a struggle isn't part of His plan, He will still make it purposeful.* If the struggle is a result of your misdirection, don't fret, God can make it work together for your good if you turn to Him.

If you don't understand the origin of your struggle, find peace in knowing, if God is behind it, the pit is part of the plan. The prison is on the path and you have help every step of the way.

Defeat is not part of the plan- a few pits maybe. Perhaps even a time or two of feeling imprisoned by struggle, but not destruction-not today; not tomorrow; not ever. You cannot be destroyed.

Fear of destruction is the enemy's go-to trick. Death is his biggest lie. Jesus defeated death and you are indestructible. "I am he that liveth, and was dead; and, behold, I am alive forevermore, Amen; and have the keys of hell and death. (Revelation 1:18)"

In Jesus, we have eternal life. We have access to a more abundant life and our result is always the Father's house with many mansions.

"For it is You who blesses the righteous man, O LORD, You surround him with favor as with a shield." Psalm –Psalm 5:12

Repeat after me, "Pit, prison, palace-giving up is not an option". A negative perspective is not an option. Wallowing in a self-PIT-y state of mind is not an option.

The pit is part of the plan. The prison is on the path and the palace is the promise. Your mission: Stay focused on the promise. Look at Joseph's own words, "Come near to me, please and they came near. And he said, 'I am your brother, Joseph, whom you sold into Egypt. And now do not be distressed or angry with yourselves because you sold me here, for God sent me before you to preserve life.'"

Trust God to give your struggle a purpose. You may be in prison today, but you have palace potential. The struggle is real, but so is your God.

When Joseph revealed his identity to his brothers, he told them, "And now, do not be distressed and do not be angry with yourselves for selling me here, because it was to save lives that God sent me ahead of you (Genesis 45:5)."

Joseph finally understood. He couldn't see the why amid the struggle, but now he understood how all of the events of his life had worked together for not only his good but the good of his family as well.

It's tough to see right now, but something in this struggle you're going through is going to prepare you. Don't distress over the tears you've shed. Don't be angry because of the betrayal you've endured. God's going to use it all.

Lessons from Joseph's Struggle

 *God is always present.

*You have favor from God that you don't know about.

*The pit is part of the plan.

*The prison is on the path to the promise.

*Every temptation comes with an escape route.

*You can be promoted from any level.

*Promotion comes from God.

*You have palace potential.

*Forgive and you will find peace.

~ * ~

~ MY PRAYER ~

HEAVENLY FATHER, you promised to surround me with favor like a shield. I want to believe that, but

I tend to focus on the negative. I don't feel supported. It's so frustrating when I look at my struggle and it seems like things are getting worse instead of better. I've tried and tried to do the right things, to take the right steps, but I don't feel like I'm making any progress.

Worse, I feel like I'm going backward. If it's not one thing it's another. One day I am up then the next day I am down and depressed. I get discouraged when I see so many people prospering while I am struggling.

Lord, I know this struggle will not last. I know you have a better plan for me. Teach me Lord your will for me in this season of my life.

Lord, I look to you for all of my help. You know me. You know my ways and my desires. You created me in my mother's womb. There is no dark place within my struggle that is hidden from you. My ears are open to hearing your voice dear Lord.

My heart is ready to receive your love and kindness. Holy Spirit comfort me when I am afraid and guide me when I take action. Father, I pray that every step I take in this season is ordered by you. As I put my trust in you, I know that you will give me joy and peace.

I trust that you will protect, guide, support, and promote me. Your word says your eyes are on me and your ears are attentive to my cry (Psalm 34:15). Help me to grow into the person that I was meant to be. As

I walk in your will, bless the works of my hands. Give me a favor in the sight of others. Teach me to lean to your understanding in times of struggles.

I can depend on you. You have never forsaken the righteous. I will lift my eyes unto the hills. All of my help comes from you.

~ TRANSFORMATIONAL SCRIPTURES ~

But I have prayed for thee, that thy faith fails not: and when thou art converted, strengthen thy brethren.

(Luke 22:32)

Examine yourselves, to see whether you are in the faith. Test yourselves. Or do you not realize this about yourselves, that Jesus Christ is in you?—unless indeed you fail to meet the test!

(2 Corinthians 13:5 ESV)

But the Lord was with Joseph and showed him steadfast love and gave him favor in the sight of the keeper of the prison. (Genesis 39:21)

The Lord is my light and my salvation-whom shall I fear? The Lord is the stronghold of my life of whom shall I be afraid? Psalm 27:1

BY HIS GRACE YOU ARE SET FREE

But by the gift of God's grace all are put right with him through Christ Jesus, who sets them free
Romans 3:24

~CHAPTER 3 ~

HE'S ZEROED IN ON YOUR STRUGGLE

(1 Kings 17)

THE STRUGGLE WAS REAL FOR THE WIDOW. She was in dire need with no clue how her needs would be met. She was the sole provider and she was struggling.

There had been a drought for three and a half years. Famine had devastated the land (Luke 4:25-26). She was stressed and losing hope. Not to mention she was probably weak from carrying the load. I can tell you, a heavy load plus limited resources equals a real struggle.

What I love most is that God saw her individually. Jesus said in Luke, that there were many widows during the famine, but she was the only widow to whom Elijah was sent.

God is sending you help. The world is struggling, but He's zeroed in on your struggle. You have His full attention. Does He have your full faith? If you're praying, your answer is on the way. Everybody you know may be struggling, but because you prayed, there's a victory heading your way. Stay faithful and keep an open mind. God's been known to provide from unlikely sources.

The widow's help came in the form of a Prophet. A man of God who had drunk from a brook and been fed by Ravens. He had his share of struggles, but God sent him to her. "Get up, go to Zarephath (which belongs to Sidon), and stay there. I've commanded a widow there to feed you." (1 King 17:9)

That's how much God trusts His children. He knows he can send you to help another because you know the struggle too. More importantly, you know He can work miracles. He needs you to testify to that. He needs you to use your struggle experience to help someone else through theirs.

God sent Elijah, who understood when the struggle is real, so is your God.

"Elijah said to her, 'Don't worry about anything. Go ahead and do what you've said.

But first, make a small biscuit for me and bring it back here. Then go ahead and make a meal from what's left for you and your son."

That's a word for anyone in a struggle, "Don't worry about anything." Go ahead with your life, putting God first, and He will deliver you out of the struggle.

God put it on her heart to help the prophet. Isn't it just like God to ask you to help someone else when you need help yourself? When you have a personal relationship with God, he speaks to you. He sees you struggling and

He sends help.

Sometimes you receive instruction before you receive the provision. I've learned when God asks me to do something that seems illogical; He's trying to get me in position to activate a principle. The widow had barely enough food, yet God instructed her to feed Elijah.

In this instance, for the widow, at least two scripture principles come to mind:

Be not deceived; God has not mocked: for whatsoever a man soweth, that shall he also reap. (Galatians 6:7)

Give and you will receive. Your gift will return to you in full--pressed down, shaken together to make room for more, running over, and poured into your lap. The amount you give will determine the amount you get back." (Luke 6:37 NLT)

The widow helped someone else during her struggle. She took her mind off of her problems; obeyed God, and blessed someone else. We can always be a blessing. No matter how we are struggling, God has blessed us all with something that can help someone else.

"One who is faithful in a very little is also faithful in much, and one who is dishonest in a very little is also dishonest in much." – Luke 16:10

She gave the little that she had. If God places it on your heart to give it away, know that He is up to something. Like the widow did in her own life, you will, by helping others, activate blessings in your own life.

"The jar of flour will not run out and the bottle of oil will not become empty before God sends rain on the land and ends this drought,'" (1 Kings 17:13-14, NIV)

She heard from God and she was obedient in her struggle. Drought or not, God does his best work when you seem to have the least to work with.

"But he said to me, "My grace is sufficient for you, for my power is made perfect in weakness." Therefore I will boast all the more gladly of my weaknesses, so that the power of Christ may rest upon me." (2 Corinthians 12:9, ESV)

Stay motivated. God has commanded a blessing just for you. Pray, listen and follow His direction. Indeed the struggle is real, but so is your God.

His eye is on the sparrow. Know that He is watching over you.

Lessons from the Widow's Struggle

* God hears your prayers.

*Help is on the way.

*Obedience activates blessings.

*God wants your blessings to overflow

*God is access to infinite supply.

~ * ~

~ MY PRAYER ~

 HEAVENLY FATHER, you said you would never leave me or forsake me. (Hebrews 13:5) Lord, I pray you will help me to believe that you are in this struggle with me.

 I admit dear Lord that I am weak, but your word says your strength is made perfect in my weakness. It feels like I am all alone, but I want to stand firm on your promise that you will never leave me.

 This struggle is difficult. I am tempted to give up. It hurts and I feel ashamed. What I am facing is bigger than me and I don't see how it's going to get better. Often I feel confused and afraid. I don't have the resources to fulfill the needs that I have. Things seem impossible. I admit that I am afraid of this struggle.

 Lord, I surrender this fear and worry to you. I receive the victory that you have planned for me.

Father, I believe that my help is coming from you. I desire to walk by faith and authority. Strengthen me oh Lord. I'm seeking you for guidance. I desire a deeper more intimate relationship with the Holy Spirit. I want to hear your word. I pray the blinders are removed from my eyes so that I can see the way.

You are a God of unlimited supply. The cattle of a thousand hills belong to you and (Psalm 50:10). Nothing is impossible for you. I believe that this struggle is temporary and that you will make every part of it work together for my good.

Father I don't want to be in this struggle. I surrender it all to you. I lean to your understanding. I pray that "out of your glorious riches, you will strengthen me with power through Your Spirit in my inner being."

Father I know if you be for me no struggle can be against me. I stand firm on your word in Matthew 7. I am asking for your provision in this struggle and I believe that you have provided it now in Jesus' name.

~ TRANSFORMATIONAL SCRIPTURES ~

I am the LORD your God, who brought you up out of the land of Egypt.

Open your mouth wide and I will fill it.

(Psalms 81:10)

You did not choose me, but I chose you and appointed you that you should go

And bear fruit and that your fruit should abide, so that whatever you ask the Father

In my name, he may give it to you. (John 15:16)

And if we know that he hears us--whatever we ask--we know

That we have what we asked of him.

(1 John 5:15)

And if we know that he hears us--whatever we ask--we know

That we have what we asked of him.

(Exodus 15:2)

IN HIS GRACE ARE MANY BLESSINGS

Out of the fullness of his grace he has blessed us all, giving us one blessing after another.

John 1:16

~ CHAPTER 4 ~

THE WALLS WILL FALL

(Joshua 6)

THE STRUGGLE WAS REAL FOR JOSHUA. His mission was to conquer the city of Jericho and his struggle was 25 ft. high, 20 ft. thick stone wall.

What struggles are you facing that seems impenetrable?

Take a step back from it. Stop trying to push against it. It's not your frail human body that will knock down the struggle, but the mighty Spirit of God within you.

"Then he said to me, "This is the word of the LORD to Zerubbabel saying, 'Not by might nor by power, but by My Spirit,' says the LORD of hosts. 7 'What are you, O great mountain? Before Zerubbabel you will become a plain; and he will bring forth the top stone with shouts of "Grace, grace to it! (Zechariah 4:6-7)

Your struggle is nothing great before the power of the Spirit. It will, in Jesus' name, be flattened and made a plain!

God promised Joshua the victory and then gave him instructions for obtaining it:

(2)But the Lord said to Joshua, "I have given you Jericho, its king, and all its strong warriors. (3) You and your fighting men should march around the town once a day for six days. (4) Seven priests will walk ahead of the Ark, each carrying a ram's horn. On the seventh day, you are to march around the town seven times, with the priests blowing the horns. (5) When you hear the priests give one long blast on the rams' horns, have all the peoples shout as loud as they can.

Then the walls of the town will collapse, and the people can charge straight into the town." Joshua 6: 1-5 (NLT)

God has already promised us the victory and He has also given us instructions, in His word, to obtain it.

Today, our confidence should be in the victory that we already have through Christ Jesus. *But in all these things we overwhelmingly conquer through Him who loved us.* (Romans 8:37)

Picture it, believers marching, trumpets blowing, and God's chosen shouting. They weren't throwing rocks or wielding sledge hammers. They were following God; circling the struggle; blowing horns and shouting! "Not by might or power, but by His spirit."

Why settle for the struggle when you can succeed by His Spirit? Just as God was with Joseph, and mindful of Widow of Zaraphath, so was He with Joshua on his mission to conquer new land.

Change can be a struggle. The struggle is real when we are faced with change. God promises He will not abandon us. We may not have to fight battles, but we face struggles every day that make us question our ability to handle the task at hand.

Walls were 25 feet high and 20 feet thick. Jericho was a symbol of military power and strength. It was considered invincible.

God told Joshua that the Jericho victory was his and gave him instructions. For six days while the trumpets blew they marched around the city. On the seventh day, they marched around seven times. On Joshua's orders, Israel shouted and the walls crumbled.

I remember when I first purchased my home. I was nervous about purchasing it because it was my first home and I was new to the process. When the underwriters came back with conditional approval,

I at first, felt defeated.

They wanted me to pay off a substantial credit card balance, before approving my loan. I was less than two weeks away from closing and I couldn't believe this was happening. I thought maybe it was a sign that I wasn't supposed to have the house.

Frustrated, I phoned my sister to vent. She and her husband offered to give me the money and told me not to worry about it. Their generosity blessed me, but I didn't want to borrow money. That night I prayed and I remembered the story of Joshua and Jericho.

I knew in my heart, this house was for me. The next morning I drove to the building site. With my hands lifted in praise I walked around my future home seven times, by faith declaring, "Not by might or power, but by His Spirit, I receive this blessing God has for me. I receive my new home, in Jesus' name."

Say What Now!?

A few days later, the bank contacted me. What they said astonishes me to this day, "Ms. Davis, for some reason, the credit card balance that we requested you to pay is no longer showing up on your credit report so legally, we cannot require you to pay it."

Say What? Since when does stuff disappear from credit reports?

In awe of God, I gave Him praise and contacted my sister with the news. We all agreed God had intervened. That's what Grace does. It intervenes.

Walls fall when we trust God's goodwill to be done. When we walk by faith and God's promises, He is faithful.

If your struggle seems insurmountable it is not. When God gets involved, the walls will fall.

#wallsWillfall

If you've enjoyed this book so far, take a moment to leave a comment for browsers who may be considering giving it a try. 😊

Lessons from Joshua's Struggle

*You won't always understand

*God comes first always

*Victory is already established

*Struggles are overcome by His Spirit

~ * ~

~ MY PRAYER ~

 HEAVENLY FATHER, I have been worried about so many things. Your word says, "All my longings lie open before you, Lord;" my sighing is not hidden from you (Psalm 38:9). I know you hear my prayers and I know you care for me.

Lead me by your Spirit. Help me to be quick to listen, slow to speak; and slow to become angry. (James 1: 19) I know the desires of my heart cannot be achieved through the flesh. I crucify my flesh and surrender to you.

 Dear Lord, go before me in my struggle and make every crooked way straight (Isaiah 45:2). Help me to stand boldly as a lion and declare *my God has already delivered me*.

 Teach me to stand firm on your word, seeking you first in all that I do. I rejoice in the face of struggle. No wall is too mighty for you to bring down.

 I hold fast in my heart the covenant of your promises for me. Father, I thank you that your word will accomplish what it is sent for to do. You have never forsaken the righteous and I know that you will not forsake me.

I will seek you early and meditate on your word day and night. I will not fear for I know you are with me to strengthen me and hold me up.

I will rejoice and magnify your name, because you have already given me the upper hand, in Jesus name, Amen.

~ TRANSFORMATIONAL SCRIPTURES ~

"For I am the Lord your God who takes hold of your right hand and says to you, do not fear; I will help you."

Isaiah 41:13

"Where can I go from your Spirit?

Where can I flee from your presence?

If I go up to the heavens, you are there;

if I make my bed in the depths, you are there.

If I rise on the wings of the dawn,

if I settle on the far side of the sea,

even there your hand will guide me,

your right hand will hold me fast.

Psalm 139:7-12

Peace I leave with you; my peace I give you.

I do not give to you as the world gives.

Do not let your hearts be troubled and do not be afraid.

- John 14:27

And God can bless you abundantly, so that in all things at all times, having all that you need, you will abound in every good work.

– Corinthians 9:8

HIS GRACE COMES WITH NO STRINGS

Let us praise God for his glorious grace, for the gift he gave us in his dear Son!
Ephesians 1:6

CHAPTER 5

IT'S NOT TOO LATE

(2 Chronicles 33: 1-20)

THE STRUGGLE WAS REAL FOR MANASSEH. *Evil*. That's the word used to describe Manasseh in scripture. He'd become king of Judah at the age of twelve after his father Hezekiah died. His father had his faults, but he had a powerful relationship with God.

Manasseh, however, was the opposite.

Manasseh was so far from God it seemed there was no turning back. Have you ever felt that way? Like you've done so much wrong, made so many mistakes that you were too far from God to turn back? It's never too late to turn back. God's love is available to you. His arms are always open, no matter how far gone you think you are. Manasseh was pretty far gone.

He worshipped idols in God's temple. He participated in the occult; sacrificed his son and shed innocent blood. 2 Kings 21:9 says, "Manasseh led the people astray so that they did more evil than the nations the Lord had destroyed before the Israelites."

Verse 16 of 2 Kings, describes how Manasseh not only provoked God himself, but he also led Judah to commit sins and do evil in the eyes of God.

What have you done that seems unforgivable?

The temptation is everywhere, but God knows that struggle very well. His promise in 1 Corinthians 10:13 is, "No temptation has overtaken you except what is common to mankind. And God is faithful; he will not let you be tempted beyond what you can bear. But when you are tempted, he will also provide a way out so that you can endure it."

God used Manasseh's capture to get his attention. "The Lord spoke to Manasseh and his people, but they ignored all his warnings. So the Lord sent the commanders of the Assyrian armies, and they took

Manasseh prisoner. They put a ring through his nose, bound him in bronze chains, and led him away to Babylon. (2 Chronicles 33:10-11)

People do change, but for some, who are deep in the bowels of sin, it may take hitting rock bottom. Manasseh could have turned back to God at any time, but he ignored all the warnings. What warnings has God given you?

Our pride can sometimes get in the way of hearing God. We don't want to be wrong. Or our sin feels so good that we think *how could this possibly be wrong*?

Idol gods please the flesh but destroy the soul. The enemy deceives people into believing that God wants them to be unhappy and miserable- that God is depriving them of something.

Don't let guilt hold you back from a relationship with God. The bible says we have all gone astray like sheep. You're not the first one who has strayed and you won't be the last. God is ready to forgive you.

The instant you repent and turn back to Him, he will restore you.

Manasseh received forgiveness and so can we. No matter how "bad" we have been God wants all to be saved. This isn't a commit-sin-free-card, but it is, for us, a reason to rejoice. God is patient and He won't give up on us, even at our worst.

"The Lord is not slow to fulfill his promise as some count slowness, but is patient toward you, not wishing that any should perish, but that all should reach repentance." (2 Peter 3:9 ESV)

God hates sin, and He was not at all pleased with Manasseh or the people (2 Kings 21:13-15). Thank God today that we have Jesus to intercede on our behalf. God sent His son Christ to die for our sins that we might be reconciled with God through Christ Jesus.

Right now, in whatever messed up state our life is in, we can repent and turn to God. It may be hard. It may be stressful and scary, but it can be done because God is waiting with open arms to help us through it.

Like Manasseh, we should humble ourselves before the one true God. Then by the grace of God, we set our lives on a path to restoration.

"But while in deep distress, Manasseh sought the Lord his God and sincerely humbled himself before the God of his ancestors. And when he prayed, the Lord listened to him and was moved by his request. So the Lord brought Manasseh back to Jerusalem and his kingdom.

Then Manasseh finally realized that the Lord alone is God!" (2 Chronicles 33:12-13).

After Manasseh turned back to God, he set things right. He rebuilt the outer wall of the City of David; removed the idols from the Lord's Temple; and restored the altar of the Lord. Life is a gift.

Every day that we live is an opportunity to repent and turn back to God. As long as we are living, it's never too late to turn back.

Lessons from Manasseh's Struggle

 *God is the one true God.

*Restoration is possible.

*Restoration begins with repentance.

*God's mercy is available for everyone.

*No sin is greater than God's love.

*God gives us signs and warnings.

~ * ~

~ MY PRAYER ~

HEAVENLY FATHER, I repent for my sins and I have chosen to turn from the ways of my past.

Your word says you've set before us life and death, blessings and cursing. I choose life. I receive your forgiveness and unconditional love.

I am choosing to trust that your perfect love will cast out all of my fears and feelings of condemnation and unworthiness.

I receive your mercy that is new for me every morning. I receive your goodness and mercy and I thank you that they are following me all the days of my life.

I have made a lot of mistakes and I haven't always respected your teachings or followed your instruction. But you are a loving and forgiving God.

You have removed my transgressions from me as far as the east is from the west (Psalm 103:12)

I receive your grace and mercy. I'm ready to turn from evil and do good; seek peace and pursue it (Psalm 34:14).

Create in me a clean heart. Every day I will serve you in Spirit and truth.

My heart desires to lay up treasures in heaven as I grow in grace and knowledge of you.

~TRANSFORMATIONAL SCRIPTURES~

There is therefore now no condemnation to them which are in Christ Jesus, who walk not after the flesh, but after the Spirit. – Romans 8:1

This is what is written: The Christ will suffer and rise from the dead on the third day, (47) And that repentance and remission of sins should be preached in his name among all nations, beginning at Jerusalem.- Luke 24:46-47

Repent ye therefore, and be converted, that your sins may be blotted out when the times of refreshing shall come from the presence of the Lord;-Acts 3:19

"I have wiped out your transgressions like a thick cloud And your sins like a heavy mist. Return to Me, for I have redeemed you." – Isaiah 44:22

Come now, and let us reason together, saith the LORD: though your sins are as scarlet, they shall be as white as snow; though they are red like crimson, they shall be as wool.

-Isaiah 1:18

IN HIS GRACE IS ETERNAL LIFE

For it is by God's grace that you have been saved through faith. It is not the result of your efforts, but God's gift, so that no one can boast about it.

Ephesians 2:8-9

~ CHAPTER 6 ~

LET THIS BITTER STRUGGLE PASS

(Matthew 26:36-46; Mark 14:32-42; Luke 22:39-46; John 18:1)

THE STRUGGLE WAS REAL FOR JESUS. Tears streamed down as Jesus prayed to His Father in heaven, "If it is your will, let this cup of suffering be removed. Yet not my will but thine be done."

Prayers and tears go hand in hand when you're in a struggle. Your struggles may not compare to Jesus'. He was brutally beaten and crucified. But your struggle is real. You feel beaten by life. You feel scorned and persecuted. You feel like people around misunderstand you and are ready to hang you on a cross.

You may not even be struggling over your problem; it may be the struggle of a child, grandchild, friend, or spouse that has you in tears.

Crying is a natural emotional response to pain. It's that time when you can't contain yourself and the inner emotions spillover. We sometimes cry when we're happy too, but in the case of struggles, tears can represent release and surrender.

Jesus, in the garden, released tears of fear and anguish. He was so filled with agony at the thought of the torture He was about to endure. It was overwhelming to him. He was God in a physical body and that physical body was struggling.

Don't feel bad when you cry or feel like you've "buckled" under pressure. You are human, but Christ lives in you and that power is greater than any struggle you face.

Meditate on Romans 6:7-12

7Now we have this treasure in jars of clay to show that this surpassingly great power is from God and not from us. **8**We are pressed on all sides, but not crushed; perplexed, but not in despair; persecuted, but not forsaken; struck down, but not destroyed.

10We always carry around in our body the death of Jesus, so that the life of Jesus may also be revealed in our body. **11**For we who are alive are always consigned to death for Jesus' sake, so that the life of Jesus may also be revealed in our mortal bodies. **12**So then, death is at work in us, but life is at work in you.

Life struggles weigh heavily on our physical bodies, but the power we need to overcome doesn't come from our earth suits. The power comes from God within us. I know that doesn't make it hurt any less. You may be wondering, *but how do I stop feeling so stressed?*

 I've found it helps me to focus on something else. Once I was so stressed that I downloaded a ton of sermons onto an mp3 player and I listened to them all day. Seriously, those earbuds were plugged in 24/7 for days.

 It was my way of staying hopeful. As long as the word was pouring into my ears continually I found that I felt better and I was more optimistic.

 Sure I would rather have had the bitter cup pass from me, but it was painfully obvious that I was going to have to go through it. It was what it was, but I had two choices: go through it kicking, screaming, and stressing or take the Lords' hand and let Him walk me through the valley.

Even Jesus temporarily broke down to the point of absolute fear and anguish. *His sweat was as drops of blood*, but even in His moment of human weakness, He gave us a model to live by.

Close your eyes and imagine, *walking through the valley of the shadows of death*, holding the Lord's hand. You wouldn't be sweating, crying, or fretting. You'd have courage. You'd be enthusiastic and certain that you were going to get through. You'd feel comfortable and safe knowing the Lord was by your side.

Jesus holding my hand is what I meditate on during every struggle; when I'm weary from well-doing; when I pray for my children; when happiness seems to be running away from me. It's the image I hold until the tests and trials I face transform into what God promised.

In scripture, Jesus prayed three times, "Father If it is possible, let this cup of suffering be taken away." Matthew 26:42 records his word this way, "My Father, if this cup can't be taken away unless I drink it, may your will be done."

He began His prayer from the desires of His flesh. Our flesh always wants to do the opposite of what we should do spiritually.

That war within us keeps us from seeing our struggles from God's perspective. We instead see situations through the eyes of fear, blinding us to the breakthroughs and victories readily available in the Spirit.

Cures to diseases and solutions to problems are all around us, but I believe we are so in the flesh about them that we cannot see or do what needs to be done. We get stuck in the flesh, but as Jesus models for us, it's okay to feel doubt, but not stay there. He shows us while starting in fear and doubt is human nature; we are not to stay there. We push through. We press toward a higher calling of faith.

Galatians 5:17, says "For the flesh lusted against the Spirit, and the Spirit against the flesh: and these are contrary the one to the other: so that ye cannot do the things that ye would."

The King James Version uses the word "lust", but read the New Living Translation:

The sinful nature wants to do evil, which is just the opposite of what the Spirit wants. And the Spirit gives us desires that are the opposite of what the sinful nature desires. These two forces are constantly fighting each other, so you are not free to carry out your good intentions.

I recall a time or two (or twenty) when I was struggling with something and my entire prayer was in fear mode. I started with, *oh God please help me* and finished with *Oh lord I can't do this. When are you coming?*

#SurrenderTheStruggle

At the end of Jesus' prayer, He said, "Not my will, but thine be done." Jesus surrendered the struggled.

That was key for me in my spiritual walk. I always held on to the struggle. I remember taking a break from writing one day and going to the park.

As I sat on the swings with my son, I looked into the sky and I prayed. *"God I just want to let go. With all my heart, I just want to surrender every struggle to you."*

I've noticed that I can say I've let go, but somehow I still feel the stress and anxiety of the struggle that I was sure that I gave to God. We're human. The heaviness of our struggles is challenging for the flesh alone to bear.

Only when we release the struggle to God and walk in the Spirit, can we truly be free? While the Spirit may be willing the flesh is weak. That's why God warns us against walking in the flesh- or living life by what we see, hear, and feel.

The worse you feel about the struggle, the further you are from walking in the Spirit. When you can get up from prayer with an attitude of not my will by God's be done, you are headed in the right direction. You haven't quite arrived because you still have to walk it out daily. I can't count the number of times I *took it to God and prayer* on Monday only to take it back in worry on Thursday.

Jesus surrendered to God's will; endured the painful journey of the cross. He remained faithful until He said, "It is finished." We have to lay our struggles on the altar. Say *Not my will, but Yours be done* and then walk by faith *until it is finished.*

The Joy That Was Set Before Him

Calvary's struggle was about to birth salvation. As the Son of God, Jesus knew full well, the joy that was set before him. He knew that He would destroy death and conquer Hell. He knew that He would destroy death and conquer Hell for all eternity. He knew that His struggle would transform life for us all.

Know this; your struggle is producing faith, patience, and perseverance. Though you are crying tears of fear and anxiety now, keep your eyes on Jesus. He is the author and finisher of your faith.

Sometimes we think we know the right path and we latch onto it with all we've got. We think, *this is how it's going to work out, or this would be the best outcome.* Even though we're struggling to make things work out the way we want them too, we persist.

Jesus released the struggle. He surrendered to God, *not my will, but thine.* Have you surrendered the struggle? Or are you holding on to it for dear life, because you believe you know what's best? Are you trying to push away the bitter cup of struggle or are you trusting that it's going to work a far greater work of glory within you?

In the midnight hours, when you are awake crying, God hears you. You're not in the garden of struggle alone. The father is with you. Regardless of how many friends have fallen asleep, God never sleeps and hears your cries for help and he has already commanded victory from your struggle.

The struggle is real, but it cannot destroy you. No struggle can keep you bound, because Jesus has set you free. Surrender the struggle to God. Jesus endured it so that you don't have to remain in it. Pray as Jesus prayed. Know that the same Father Jesus prayed to is available and listening for your cries today. Pray, *not my will in this struggle, Lord, but yours be done.*

Stand on the promises of the word, "The LORD hears those who cry out, and he delivers them from all their distress." (Psalm 34:17)

God has given you the power to overcome every struggle. His goodness and mercy are following you every step of the way.

Because of the joy awaiting Jesus, he endured the cross, disregarding its shame. Now he is seated in the place of honor beside God's throne. –Hebrews 12:2

There is joy awaiting you. Stand firm on the word. Be steadfast and unmovable until *it is finished.*

#ItIsFinished

~ LESSONS FROM JESUS' STRUGGLE ~

*Friends are wonderful blessings,

but sometimes it's going to be just you and God.

*We can find strength in the struggle

through daily prayer and spending time with God.

*Power to overcome struggles comes from the God power within,

Not from the physical strength of our flesh and bones.

*It's the joy of the victory that is set before you that will encourage

and motivate you to move forward when you'd much rather give up.

~ MY PRAYER ~

Heavenly Father, TEACH ME TO
SURRENDER MY STRUGGLES.

I don't want to carry these burdens. My
spirit is willing, but my flesh is weak. I want
to release my burdens to you. Help me Lord
to let go and trust you with all of my heart.

I take your yoke upon me and I learn of
you. You said your yoke is easy and your
burdens are light. I release this burden into
your hands. Your word says that I should
cast my cares on you because you care for
me.

Let your peace that surpasses all
understanding fill my heart and mind.

Thank you, Father, angels that are assigned
to me in this struggle. I know, dear Lord that
your strength is made perfect in my
weakness. I know this suffering is
developing perseverance. You are faithful
and you will not let me be tempted beyond
what I can bear, but you will provide me a
way to escape it.

Thank you, Jesus. You endured the
struggles of the cross just for me. Your

sacrifice gave me life and life more abundantly. Your sacrifice gave me healing and set me from bondage. You have overcome the world and because of you,

I overcome every struggle. As I abide in you and you in me, I receive my victory by faith. I receive divine strength. I walk by faith and trust in a higher understanding than my own. Not my will, but God's be done.

This struggle is finished. I surrender it all, in Jesus' name, Amen.

TRANSFORMATIONAL SCRIPTURES

And Jesus answered and said unto him, Get thee behind me, Satan: for it is written, Thou shalt worship the Lord thy God, and him only shalt thou serve. –Luke 4:8

Jesus saith unto him, I am the way, the truth, and the life: no man cometh unto the Father, but by me. –John 14:16

And so I tell you, keep on asking, and you will receive what you ask for. Keep on seeking, and you will find. Keep on knocking, and the door will be opened to you. For everyone who asks, receives. Everyone who seeks finds. And to everyone who knocks, the door will be opened. -Luke 11:9-10

Jesus said unto him if thou canst believe, all things are possible to him that believeth. – Mark 9:23

And Jesus answered and said, Verily I say unto you, no man hath left the house, or brethren, or sisters, or father, or mother, or wife, or children, or lands, for my sake, and the gospels,

-Mark 10:29

An angel appeared to strengthen Jesus; praying in agony and fervently; Jesus' sweat became like drops of blood; Jesus fell on the ground to pray; (Luke 22:39-46 and John 18:1)

HIS GRACE IS FOR EVERYONE

May the grace of the Lord Jesus be with everyone.
Revelation 22:21

~ CHAPTER 7 ~

THANK GOD I SEE

(The book of Job)

The Bible describes Job as "the greatest man among all the people of the East". He was a wealthy man and considered blameless and upright. Yet, he experienced some of the most terrible struggles known to man. In the end, though, he came to several conclusions that led him to the greatest story of struggle and supernatural turnaround of all time.

He is (to me) the ultimate example of a comeback success story. The conclusions are lessons we can still benefit from today.

Systematically, the enemy attacked every aspect of Jobs' life. The first time the enemy targeted Job's children and livestock, but Job refused to curse God. So on the second attempt, the enemy took another approach, this time attacking Job's health.

Twice he came after job. His wanted Job to lose all faith in God. That's the goal with you. He wants you to lose your faith because faith is the one thing that can hold you together when you feel like falling apart.

You might be worn out; grief-stricken and tired, but as the song says, *long as I've got King Jesus, I don't need anybody else.*

To this day, the enemy tries the same schemes with the children of God. He tries to get to us through our children; our finances; our spouses; and our health and even our friends.

According to scripture says Job was speechless. For seven days, he was at a complete loss for words. He lay on the ground defeated, confused and angry. His body covered, from head to heels, with painful boils and blisters.

Job's wife told him to just get it over with-curse God and die. People love to tell you what you should do. They see your struggle from the outside and to them, it looks hopeless. And even though it would be easier to just give up, something in you still can't give up on God. You know too much about His goodness and His mercy to believe that He would let you die in the struggle.

The enemy:

Killed his entire livestock (Finances).

Murdered his children (family).

Drive a wedge between Job and his wife (Spouse).

Put him at odds with his friends (Relationships).

Covered him with boils (Health)

The struggle was real for Job. I wouldn't wish a struggle this severe on my worst enemy. There something we have to remember about Job's struggle.

God knew exactly what was happening. He knew every step the enemy was going to make. And He knew how much Job could handle. God is **Omniscient**. He knows all-past, present, and future. He knew Job and He knows you.

Our Father understands our struggles, but He also knows how much we can take. He created us in His image and so we can be confident in 1 Corinthians 10:13, "There hath no temptation taken you but such as is common to man: but God is faithful, who will not suffer you to be tempted above that ye are able; but will with the temptation also make a way to escape, that ye may be able to bear it."

Job finally reached a point where he felt utterly defeated. Scripture says he cursed the day that he was born. He was so bad off that he wished he'd never been born. Have you ever felt that defeated, letdown, or rejected. Where the pain and agony of your breaking heart were so unbearable that you just wished you'd never existed?

Take heart, my friend. The Lord is your refuge and your fortress; your God, trust in Him. Surely He will deliver you from the snare of the fowler and the perilous pestilence. Psalm 91: 2-3(NKJV)

Jobs Children

If there is a child in your life that you love dearly, then you can relate to Jobs, constant prayers for his children. God blesses us with children, and much to our chagrin, they have their minds and what to live their own lives.

My greatest struggles have involved my children. They've kept me praying for the night and day. They are always on your mind and in your heart. Our heart desires to protect them and keep them safe, but we can't be with them every minute of the day.

I can't even pretend to understand Job's loss and I highly respect the men and women who do. Recently, I received an email from a reader who'd lost her son.

She was so full of hope and encouragement. Her words were amazing. Her strength reminded me of Job. She'd endured one of the greatest struggles known to a parent, yet she still gave God the praise- simply *amazing*.

My kids haven't always done exactly as I want them to, but my prayers and faith, have made a tremendous difference. I can testify to that. If your struggle is about your children, remember, God has given us promises to stand on:

In Isaiah 54:13, God will bring peace to our children.

In Isaiah 49:25-26, God will fight for and save our children.

In Psalm 103:17, God will increase our children more and more.

In Proverbs 14:26, our children have refuge in the Lord.

Since writing this book, I'm renewing my habit of praying these (and others) blessings regularly over my sons and now my granddaughter. God's word will not return void. Nothing can separate them from God's love and nothing should separate them from our loves.

Even though Job feared his children's behavior, he still prayed for his kids regularly. The prayers of parents and caregivers are powerful. Pray, parent your best, and let God handle the rest.

Scripture says Job prayed and made sacrifices for his children daily. Remember when God mentioned Job, the enemy said, Job has a hedge around him.

I often pray a hedge of protection around my children, family, and home. With each prayer, I believe, that the hedge grows stronger and stronger.

God's protection can be so strong in your life, that even enemies will take notice of the blessing of how things seem to always work out for you.

The Dangerous Assumptions Jobs Friends Made About His Struggle

When it comes to taking advice, my advice is- take the good stuff that sounds helpful and let the rest blow in the wind. Fan it off like you would a hot bean burrito fart. Did I just say that? Yep.

Go ahead and laugh. The bible says a cheerful heart is a good medicine (Proverbs 17:22).

Speaking of farts, Job's three friends, Eliphaz, Bildad, and Zophar released plenty of hot air concerning Job's situation.

People have a lot to say when it's you, but when it's their business up for discussion, they shut down and turn into Fort Knox. They let nothing out and you can't get any advice in. Oh, but when it's your struggle in the limelight.

You Know What They Say About Assumptions

All three of Jobs' friends made this same assumption- Job had sinned against God and the Lord was punishing him. They couldn't fathom any other reason for Job's suffering.

This is a natural reaction when we go through struggles, surely God must be punishing us for our sins.

There are consequences for sins, but in response to this false assumption, Job's friend Elihu asked several fantastic questions in chapter 35:5-8:

"Look up at the heavens and see; gaze at the clouds so high above you. If you sin, how does that affect him? If your sins are many what does that do to him? If you are righteous, what do you give to him or what does he receive from your hand? Your wickedness affects only a man like yourself, and your righteousness only the sons of men."

The assumption that God is more concerned with our sin than our salvation is one false assumption that we still make today.

When we see people go through tough times, we wonder, with our limited reasoning, *why* and with all of our earthly wisdom and knowledge the only thing we can come up with is, *they've done something wrong.*

Job's friend Bildad had the nerve to say, "if you are pure and upright, surely He will rouse himself up on your behalf and restore you to your rightful place." (8:6)

As if to say, *if you're so perfect, God wouldn't let you suffer.*

Poor judgmental fella- he's the type to run his mouth and speak his mind when he should be quiet because his brain is running out of gas and about to shut down at any moment.

Little did Job's "friend", Bildad, know and **less** do your friends know; Job was upright in the sight of God and you are righteous in Christ Jesus.

Bildad was speaking out of turn as my granny would say. He had no idea what he was talking about. You have to be careful when you listen to friends about your struggles.

They laid down some serious bible-thumping- guilt-tripping advice when the truth of the matter as; was; Job was being tested at God's consent.

People don't always know what God is doing in your life any more than you do. Don't take their comments so seriously.

Stuck In A Loop of Struggle

I've made the same assumptions in my own life. I was so well acquainted with my mistakes, that whenever I struggled, I made a habit of tracing it to sin.

Never mind that I'd already repented and asked God to forgive me. But because of my limited thinking, I continued to punish myself for what I'd done wrong and on some level decided that it was okay if God wanted me to suffer for it.

God doesn't want us to suffer. The fear and self-doubt that we feel aren't coming from Him. He wants to heal those scars, not pour salt in them. Just because I haven't let go doesn't mean God is still holding.

I had to forgive myself. I had to stop shaming myself and beating myself up with, "I should have known better than that."

Job repented in chapter 42. He confessed and was restored. Immediately, Job received the restoration he needed. We know that because scripture says Job's health returned; he received twice as much real estate and cattle; he had more children, and lived a long life.

Had Job simply wallowed in his mistakes, he couldn't have been restored. He was done struggling. Enough was enough. His restoration had to begin in his heart, from His knowledge of who God is and what God desired for him.

Job even forgave his friends for their bad advice and interceded on their behalf just as he'd done in the past for his children.

We Have No Idea what's going on.

The main takeaway for me in this chapter is this; it's okay when we don't know why. There is a song we sang in the Primitive Baptist church that said, "We'll understand it better by and by".

Stop bullying yourself. Repent, receive your restoration. God is ready to rebuild your life, but you have to make the choice to receive restoration by faith.

It's easy to get caught in a loop of repenting and feeling guilty, but never receiving the restoration. Have you received your restoration or are you stuck in the loop of struggle?

Isaiah 50:17 encourages, "For the Lord GOD helps Me, Therefore, I am not disgraced; Therefore, I have set my face like flint, and I know that I will not be ashamed."

The day we confessed and repented, we were restored. If we still struggle with a past mistake, it's because we haven't made the choice to receive or forgiven ourselves.

A Testimony of Restoration

Job's story was a little unsettling for me in earlier years, because I believed that as long as we were "perfect" Christians that nothing bad could happen to us. As long as we followed the Ten Commandments and lived a good life, we'd bypass trials and hard times.

God has never promised that we would not have challenges, He did, however; promise to help us get through them. He also promised that He would restore us.

Isaiah 1:18 says, "Come now, let us reason together, says the LORD: though your sins are like scarlet, they shall be as white as snow; though they are red like crimson, they shall become like wool."

By the end of Job's experience, he finally understood that his struggle had nothing to do with his money or how good or bad he had been. God had permitted Job to be tested.

Job made a mistake during this test that I have made. He accused God. He blamed God for the struggles that He experienced. While God allowed the struggle, He was not the destroyer. God allowed the test, but He put limits on what the enemy could do.

The LORD said to Satan, "Very well, then, he is in your hands; but **you must spare his life**." (Job 2:6)

God knows what's happening in your life. It may be the result of a series of decisions or tests of your faith, but whatever the reason you are struggling now, know this: God has placed limits on just how far that struggle can go.

~LESSONS FROM JOB'S STRUGGLE

*God always has more faith in us then we have in ourselves.

*Struggling is no indication of sin.

*Trials are a part of this life. Don't turn on God-turn toward Him.

*People will speculate, but only God knows 100% who, what, when, where, and why.

*You will never lose more than God can restore.

~ TRANSFORMATIONAL SCRIPTURES ~

*2 Chronicles 15:7- "But you, be strong and do not lose courage, for there is a reward for your work."

*Jeremiah 29:13- And ye shall seek Me, and find Me, when ye shall search for Me with all your heart."

*James 1:2-18 (ESV) Count it all joy, my brothers, when you meet trials of various kinds, for you know that the testing of your faith produces steadfastness.

*Psalm 8:4 -What is a man that you are mindful of him, the son of man that you care for him?

*John 16:33- I have told you these things, so that in me you may have peace.

In this world, you will have trouble. But take heart! I have overcome the world."

~MY PRAYER ~

Dear Lord, thank you for your grace and loving-kindness. You said if I seek you with my whole heart, I will find you (Jeremiah 29:13). I am seeking you this very moment Lord.

Thank you for your compassion that is abundant towards me. You know what I am facing. I cannot succeed apart from you. Build my strength as I go through this struggle. I desire to walk worthy of your calling. My heart is open to receive your guidance and direction.

I know you can do all things and no plan of yours can be thwarted (Job 2:2). Thing is happening that I do not fully understand and at this time I lean to you.

Be a shield around me, bestow glory on me, and lift my head (Psalm 1:4). Deliverance comes from you and I pray your hand of blessing will bring restoration.

You are my refuge and my stronghold in times of trouble. (Psalms 9:9) I will remain steadfast in my faith until this struggle is over. Even in this struggle, I will sing your praises.

Because I know that you are faithful and I believe that you have already established my restoration. My latter days will be greater. I give you honor and glory. And I will continue to praise you with my whole heart.

Fill me with all joy and peace in believing, so that by the power of the Holy Spirit I may abound in hope. **(Romans 15:13)**

Father, I know that you will put a new song in my heart. I receive the victory now, in Jesus' name, Amen.

HIS GRACE BUILDS YOU UP

And now I commend you to God and to the word of his grace, which can build you up and give you the inheritance among all those who are sanctified.

Acts 20:32

~CHAPTER 8 ~

SUCCESS LEAVES CLUES

"Though He may slay me, yet will I hope in Him"

(Job 13:15).

THE STRUGGLE *IS* REAL, BUT WITH GOD's GRACE THINGS ARE POSSIBLE. I've heard, "Success leaves clues." I believe that. When we want to be successful, we can study successful people. Hebrews 6:12 says, "Follow those who through faith and patience have obtained the promises."

The International Standard Version says, "Then, instead of being lazy, you will imitate those who are inheriting the promises through faith and patience."

I don't know about you, but I don't like to be called lazy, but I've had to admit to myself that accepting the struggle is real as if there is no hope is - *lazy faith.*

If I can't get up off my faith, follow Godly examples and overcome the struggle through faith and patience, then I'm going to remain struggling for a long-long time.

Though He Slays Me

Job is the perfect example of *money can't buy happiness* -nor health or healthy well-adjusted children. Now money can help. I'm the first to say I'd rather be rich and stressed than broke and stressed. After years of confusion on the subject, I know God has no problem with me being wealthy; money is the least of His riches.

Faith is your greatest wealth. It can change anything. You can be sick and have faith and be made whole. You can be broke and have faith and be made financially prosperous. You could be struggling so bad you want to shut down and climb under a rock until Jesus returns, but if you have faith the size of a mustard seed, you can speak to that struggle with confidence, *be thou removed and cast into the sea!*

Friend, never underestimate your faith or the power of God's grace to get you through a struggle. I've had a lot of bad stuff happen in my life. Some resulted from my crazy decisions, other things at the hands of others. I didn't always understand why and it hurt like crazy.

Job suffered incredible loss and pain. Not only that, he was humiliated and rejected by the people closest to him, all the while thinking that God was responsible for his suffering. BUT Job still said, "Though He slays me, yet will I trust Him."

I thank God, though; I have something Job didn't have. I have the power of Christ's blood working in my life. I have the blessed assurance that Jesus came that I might have life and have it more abundantly. I don't have to guess whether or not God is punishing me, because He told me in His word that His plans are not to harm me but to give me a future and hope.

When I go through struggles, I don't spend my energy wailing and crying, *why me* anymore. I don't focus on speculations or probabilities. Job's friends thought they were right. The bible says there is a way that seems right to a man but the end is destruction.

If you're facing a struggle and you have no idea why the best thing to do is meditate on scriptures. My favorite one is Psalm 34:19-

20 -A righteous man may have many troubles, but the Lord delivers him from them all; he protects all his bones, not one of them will be broken.

Forgiveness Brings Restoration

"And now, do not be distressed and do not be angry with yourselves for selling me here, because it was to save lives that God sent me ahead of you (Genesis 45:5)."

There's so much strength of character in Joseph's statement above, *"do not be angry with yourselves"*.

When you know God uses every circumstance, you don't need to hold a grudge.

Joseph was the one mistreated and betrayed, yet here he was consoling them. In Joseph's dreams, he had dominion over the struggle. God gave us dominion and authority over struggles.

We may lose some friends by speaking faith, but that's okay. The result will be a palace experience. Regardless of the pain that comes, keep the faith and never cease to pray. Know that God's Grace is yours and the struggle has an expiration date.

Little children, you are from God, and have conquered them; for the one who is in you is greater than the one who is in this world. (1 John 4:4)

Christ came to conquer the struggle and solidify your path to success. He sweated drops like blood in the garden-so much pain and all for our gain. When there is part of your brain telling you that you're going to die in your struggle, remember the devil is a liar.

Christ as overcome the world. Death has no power over you. God sees the struggle and He has placed limits on just how far it can go in your life. Stand on faith, *not your will but God's be done.*

Speak life. Pray without ceasing and know that joy and victory are set before you.

Thou, O Lord, according to thy great goodness hast promised repentance and forgiveness to them that have sinned against thee: and of thine infinite mercies hast appointed repentance unto sinners, that they may be saved.

Forgive Yourself and Move On

Manasseh understood God's forgiving nature. For all of his unrighteous and rebellious behavior, he still knew that He had a chance. He knew that God's mercy and grace were still available for him.

No struggle of sin or rebellion is beyond the blood of Jesus.

Not mine, not yours, not Manasseh's. His struggle ended with success because he, by faith repented and received God's forgiveness.

When we trust God, the anxiety and fear of struggle vanish in the presence of His love. Nothing can separate us from God's love.

It seems like it would be better to skip the droughts and bypass the prisons altogether, but our ways are not His ways.

The people we've discussed successfully overcame the struggle. Collectively they all had things in common:

They Heard From God

They Followed Directions To The Letter

They Trusted Beyond Their Ability

The Let Go of The Struggle and Grabbed On To Grace

When you follow God's instructions, walls fall; prisons lead to palaces, and needs are met in abundance.

I've tried to do things my way in the past. I've modified the word to fit my agenda and let me tell you, it didn't work out well.

For six days, while the trumpets blew, the Israelites marched around Jericho's wall.

On the seventh day they marched around seven times; blew the horns; shouted, and the walls crumbled. Talk about specific instructions.

Products labeled, assembly required, come with instructions. How many of us have trouble following those simple directions.

How many of us follow them at all. Or do you wait until you spend hours putting something together incorrectly and then you pull out the directions?

Save yourself the heartache. When it comes to matters of the Spirit, DIY is not a good thing. We should read the word and follow it then it is to follow our plan and end up with a mess.

Divine Direction

So what are some examples of scriptures that give us directions for success in life today?

.

Directions Related to Our Bodies

Or do you not know that your body is a temple of the Holy Spirit within you, whom you have from god? You are not your own, for you were bought with a price. So glorify god in your body. **(Corinthians 6:19-20)**

Do not be wise in your own eyes; fear the LORD and shun evil. [8] This will bring health to your body and nourishment to your bones. (Proverbs 3:7-8)

Directions Related to Relationships

Judge not, that you be not judged. 2 for with the judgment you pronounce you will be judged, and with the measure, you use it will be measured to you. (**Matthew 7:1-2)**

The second is this: 'Love your neighbor as yourself.' There is no commandment greater than these." (Mark 12:31)

Be completely humble and gentle; be patient, bearing with one another in love. 3 Make every effort to keep the unity of the Spirit through the bond of peace. (Ephesians 4:2-3)

Directions Related to Success

Sow seed in the morning and do not be idle in the evening, for you do not know whether morning or evening sowing will succeed, or whether both of them alike will be good. (Ecclesiastes 11:6)

Blessed is the one who does not walk in step with the wicked or stand in the way that sinners take or sit in the company of mockers,[2] but whose delight is in the law of the LORD, and who meditates on his law day and night. [3] That person is like a tree planted by streams of water, which yields its fruit in season and whose leaf does not wither—whatever they do prospers. (Psalm 1:1-3)

Commit to the LORD whatever you do, and he will establish your plans. (Proverbs 16:3)

God's direction is always available. Listen to sermons and teachings. Read your bible; spiritual growth books and bible study lessons. Ask the Holy Spirit to give you understanding and perseverance.

~People who overcome struggles, understand the importance of following divine direction. ~

Trusting Beyond Your Ability

Trusting God completely means we put aside our agenda. Imagine if Joseph had become resentful, angry, or vengeful because of His struggle. He might have cut himself off from God's favor.

He might have self-sabotaged His victory. Proverbs 3:5 encourages us to, "Trust in the LORD with all thine heart; and lean not unto thine own understanding.

God knows your heart. He knows if you intend to follow Him or your selfish motives. "But, I the Lord, search all hearts and examine secret motives. I give all people their due rewards according to what their actions deserve." Motives matter to God.

Elijah was sent to the Widow because God had commanded her to feed him. The Widow could have looked at her dire circumstance and doubted God's instructions.

She could have said no to the prophet, in which case they could have starved to death after their last meal or Elijah could have left and not been there to pray for her son who died.

So take courage, men, because I trust God that it will turn out just as he told me. (Acts 27:25)

No temptation has waylaid you that is beyond man's power; trust God, he will never let you be tempted beyond what you can stand, but when temptation comes, he will provide the way out of it, so that you can bear up under it. (1 Corinthians 10:13 ISV)

The LORD recompense thy work, and a full reward is given thee of the LORD God of Israel, under whose wings thou art come to trust. (Ruth 2:12)

As for God, his way is perfect; the word of the LORD is tried: he is a buckler to all them that trusts in him. (2 Samuel 22:31)

Had the Widow not followed God's direction, the ending would have been quite different. But her reward came as a result of her obedience and trust.

We too will overcome every struggle by trusting God completely even when we think we have a better way.

Surrender the Struggle

As I was finishing up this book, I asked myself an important question, *have I been glorifying God or the struggle?*

Scripture says, "No man can serve two masters; he will either hate the one or love the other."

That's something for me to think about the next time I open my mouth to speak about my challenges or post a status on social media.

Who am I serving?

Take the stand with me, "As for me and my house we will serve the Lord."

Let's surrender the struggle in faith to the God who knows all. Let's choose to see the struggle as an opportunity.

Not by putting on blinders and pretending that the struggle isn't real, but by walking by faith, not by sight and believing that no struggle is greater than God's grace and love for us.

Take your authority in the earth to tread on the serpent, scorpions and all manner of evil in the earth (Luke 10:19). Make it your main desire to serve God even in periods of struggle. God will not be mocked. The faith you sow will reap victory.

Draw Confidently Toward the Throne of Grace

The struggle is real, but God's grace is *ALWAYS* sufficient for us. It takes courage to let go of the struggle and grab on to Grace, but we can do it by His grace.

That's the only way. The victory begins within. It begins by knowing with your whole heart that God loves you enough to equip you with whatever you need to get through the struggle that you are in.

Draw near to god in your struggle, Hebrews 4:16:

Tells us to "confidently draw near to the throne of grace, that we may receive mercy and find grace to help in time of need.

When you have confidence, you're sure. You have that Hebrew boys swagger. You don't even need to explain why you trust god the way you do. You just do and that's all there is to it.

When you confidently draw near to the throne of grace, you have divine intervention faith. You know that God is going to do something supernatural that can blow your mind and the minds of every critic.

It took Job some time, but he confidently drew near to god. He realized that the test he endured, wad not because God was angry or punishing him, but because God had more faith in him than he had himself. And his result was double for his struggle.

Your restoration is certain. Put your struggle on the altar of grace and leave it there until you can say, like Jesus said, it is finished.

God bless.

If you enjoyed this book, please take a moment to leave a comment for browsers who may be considering giving it a try. Thank you!

Sign up for free eBook notices by entering your email here.

Popular Titles:

Deliver me from negative self talk a guide to speaking faith-filled words

Renewing your mind: mindset for victorious living

How god sees your struggles